MARTIAL ARTS MINISTRY:

*How To Start
A Martial Arts Ministry*

BY:

JOHN BLACKMAN

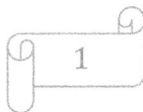

Special Request

Thank you for purchasing our book and supporting our Ministry. We have a Special Request for those that have purchased this book on the Kindle platform. We wanted to make you aware that Amazon's Kindle platform pays, "per pages read". Our Special Request is that if you appreciate our Ministry's efforts to put out books such as this, or if you would simply like to support our Ministry's work to please scroll to the back of the book, even if you don't "read" the book right away. This is how we will get paid through the paid per pages read criteria.

We all lead such busy lives nowadays and can get side tracked so easily, please take a moment to support us now by allowing us to be paid by scrolling to the end of the book – Then go back and read it at your leisure.

We deeply appreciate Your support and know that God will Bless You as You have Blessed this Ministry.

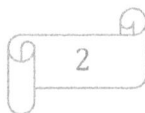

Dedication

This book is dedicated to all the Christian martial arts instructors that seek after truth and righteousness while discipling students in the faith. This book is dedicated to the Christian martial artists who follows the Word of God and not the words of men, religion, and popular culture. This book is dedicated to the Christian martial arts instructor who boldly proclaims the Word of God without compromise, without apology, and courageously stands in the gap. God Bless You!

Forward

This book may be controversial to the church establishment or even band by your local church because we expose the majority of American churches out there as "sellouts" and on the take of the government. If one of the ultimate goals for a Martial Arts Ministry is to disciple believers in the faith, this reality has to be exposed to be successful at starting a Martial Arts Ministry. The man of God who has been called to start a Martial Arts Ministry has to understand the serious nature of his responsibilities and move as the Spirit of God leads. Yet understand this, if you are speaking the truth in love as times get even darker the so-called church will turn against you - your responsibility is to think for yourself and learn directly from God

"We're all the sum of our actions – taken or not." AJF 11:34pm 08/08/2016

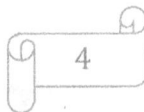

Move with a sense of urgency and purpose in love – Souls are hanging in the balance right now!

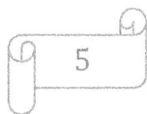

Table of Contents

Chapter 1: My Story

The Story of my Martial Arts Ministry and the means in which it was developed actually center a lot around my actual testimony of coming to know the living God in a real powerful way and accepting Jesus into my heart as my personal Lord and Savior.

Okay, so here's some background information on me. I grew up on the East Coast of the United States in Baltimore, Maryland. I grew up a Catholic not really understanding the details of the religion just understanding Jesus is good the devil is bad. By age 4 I had survived three open-heart surgeries and shortly thereafter my mother and father got divorced.

Growing up in a single parent home was challenging to say the least. My mom ended up having to go on the system so that the basic necessities of life were provided for.

As time progressed and I was about nine years old mom had another child with someone that she was a long-term relationship with. However shortly thereafter the relationship continued to dissolve until finally they separated.

It was about this time that my mom attempted to reenter the workforce. Grandma would always help out whenever she could, and whenever she knew that there was an actual need – I really miss her. Nevertheless as my mom reenter the workforce I was given the responsibility at a young age to watch my younger brother.

The combination of this responsibility coupled with the normal teenager challenges such as falling in love for the first time was a lot for me to deal with. Not to go to deep here but it's important to mention that one of the first girls that I ever, "fell in love with" was actually pregnant prior to us going out. She informed me about the dynamics and that her mother an ultraliberal was forcing her to have an abortion even though she didn't want to have one.

Now at this time I'm still a Catholic and I haven't read the Bible for myself but as I attempted to save the child's life by talking to this young lady we looked to the Bible for answers. In fact I recall her reading Scripture to me over the phone. It was a difficult situation made worse by the fact that it was a long distance relationship.

Ultimately the forces of darkness prevailed in this case and she ended up having the abortion. This experience left a profound impact on my life and a desire to protect life in every and any way possible that I could. Each of us must learn the value of life and develop the highest regard for human life and give it the proper dignity and respect that it deserves since we are in fact created in the image of God.

As I mention this situation had tremendous impact on my life, and at the time was the tipping point if you would for me to withdraw from school. I ended up dropping out after completing but not passing the 10th grade.

It was shortly after this time in my life that I began my journey into Martial Arts. A buddy of mine at the time and I were returning to his house to take a break from whatever we were doing. It was during this time that I met his sister's boyfriend who would end up being my first instructor. In the brief encounter I had with him that day he taught me a handful of skills that of course I immediately "shared" with my younger brother.

It was actually Martial Arts that God used as a tool to lead me into a new life filled with hope and love. My training was quite unique to say the least, some might even call it abusive. However, God led me to the core principles behind everything that I was being taught, opening my eyes to gain revelations on tactics, combat, and strategy. In fact God was teaching me much more than a Martial Art He was teaching me a way of life.

I'm sure some of you out there may be curious as to what particular style or system of Martial Arts that I was being trained in. Well the answer to that question in the most simple and basic terms would be one word, "Ninjutsu". Yet even answering the question here leaves room for a whole lot of assumptions and speculations, as many do not know anything about real Ninjutsu. However, that is a subject for another book in and of itself in the future.

When I was 19 things started to get interesting in my life, as if things hadn't been interesting enough already. I ended up working with my cousin in Baltimore City delivering construction type vehicles such as Bobcats to people throughout the area.

One day as I was working my old instructor came in to the shop, I think he might've been delivering sodas and snacks for the vending machine. This wasn't by chance. You see he had moved as did I. Unfortunately given the dynamics of our lives at the time we didn't stay in contact.

Nevertheless it was God once again utilizing the Martial Arts as a tool to draw me closer to Him. Now make no mistake about it this instructor was by no means a Christian. See God was using the Martial Arts as a tool, not necessarily the instructor.

It was about the same time that I learned of another gentleman that I was working with, a former Marine also practiced the same Martial Art. Again God was using Martial Arts to draw me closer to Him – what an awesome God we serve.

You see it was because this man had trained in the same Martial Arts that I did that I was receptive to what he had to say.

One day he informed me that we live in three different realms at the same time, the physical, the spiritual, and the eternal. This very much intrigued me and I pondered on this for quite some time. After that he handed me a small King James Version Bible. He lets me know that if I have any questions along the way as I read it to come back to him so we can discuss things. At this point in my life I didn't back down from challenges and regardless of whether I knew it or not at the time I was seeking truth out. Now I had said the sinners prayer once or twice after watching CBN but never took it any further – well at least until I was given that Bible.

As I began to read the Bible I started to understand that certain things within the Catholic religion went completely against what the Word of God says. I'm not going to get into all the details of that, this is not the purpose of this book but if you read the Bible with an open mind and open heart seeking truth are going to find it.

So had a choice before me, what do I believe? My own religion says that the Bible was completely and totally absolutely true, yet as I read the Bible it's telling me certain things about my religion are completely wrong. And honestly wasn't a hard choice to make, I chose the Bible – and still choose the Bible regardless of public opinion or what's socially acceptable at a given point in time.

As I began to learn and grow more I spent approximately a week on my couch, "shedding the world" is what I call it – crying out to God on my knees and repentance for the things that I've done and all that Jesus Christ has done for me. The amount of appreciation and gratitude I felt was overwhelming – this was the beginning of my walk with God.

As I began to learn, grow, and mature God put it on my heart to develop an organization that teaches self-defense methods to protect life and promote American Christian values. One of the main things that God pressed upon my heart was to prepare those that He entrust to me for these last days. So moving forward in faith I started the process.

To say everything went smoothly would be a complete fabrication and lie – you have to remember that as you move forward in faith you will face resistance from the enemy. You also must understand that the majority of the time that the enemy comes against you, to tempt you, and to war against you will be when you are at your weakest. It's important for you to plan for that, prepare for that, and be ever vigilant in your mind and in your spirit so that away you can stand in your flesh.

One of the things God had led me to do was literally to develop a Christian Ninjutsu Martial Art. This may sound like a complete backwards idea that is incompatible with one another, yet I would surmise those assuming such things do not know the true essence of Ninjutsu.

So not only did God call me to create a Christian Martial Arts Ministry, He call me to create a Christian Martial Arts style -not an easy task by any stretch of the imagination, but if God be for me who can be against me? And it is in His power and in His name, the holy name of Jesus that I continue to move forward even this very day.

In the following chapters I will lay out the foundational groundwork that I've already developed and pray that the Lord our God would enable you to be a living vessel read by all men for His glory sake, and prayerfully use Martial Arts to draw those lost souls into the Kingdom of God.

Chapter 2: Biblical Justification of Self-Defense

God has Obligated You

The Word God makes a very clear we have a Biblical obligation to protect and to promote life. Throughout the Scriptures God makes it very clear – we are to stand in the gap. Below are a handful Scriptures that you can draw upon:

Eze. 33:6 - But if the watchman see the sword come, and blow not the trumpet, and the people be not warned; if the sword come, and take any person from among them, he is taken away in his iniquity; but his blood will I require at the watchman's hand.

Psalm 82:4 Deliver the poor and needy: rid them out of the hand of the wicked.

Proverbs 24:11 - If thou forbear to deliver them that are drawn unto death, and those that are ready to be slain;

Deut. 22:8 - When thou buildest a new house, then thou shalt make a battlement for thy roof, that thou bring not blood upon thine house, if any man fall from thence.

Exodus 21:29 - But if the ox were wont to push with his horn in time past, and it hath been testified to his owner, and he hath not kept him in, but that he hath killed a man or a woman; the ox shall be stoned, and his owner also shall be put to death.

Buying and Carrying a Sword

Luke 22:35-39 - And he said unto them, When I sent you without purse, and scrip, and shoes, lacked ye any thing? And they said, Nothing. [36] Then said he unto them, But now, he that hath a purse, let him take it, and likewise his scrip: and he that hath no sword, let him sell his garment, and buy one.

[37] For I say unto you, that this that is written must yet be accomplished in me, And he was reckoned among the transgressors: for the things concerning me have an end. [38] And they said, Lord, behold, here are two swords. And he said unto them, It is enough. [39] And he came out, and went, as he was wont, to the mount of Olives; and his disciples also followed him.

As we can see here Jesus himself commands his disciples to purchase weapons. Obviously not to be offensive in nature but for self-defense purposes. The possession of weapons and skills with weapons were considered good and useful for protecting His people according to Scripture.

Warnings concerning self-defense

As we can see from Scripture the Bible makes it very clear that we have an obligation to protect life but the Bible also makes very clear not to trust solely in the sword but in the Lord Our God.

Furthermore it's imperative that we develop an intuitive and instinctual understanding through the Spirit of God for when to actually use our self-defense tactics. Looking at things clearly there is obviously a need to utilize your self-defense techniques during a life-threatening situation.

However, the goal of any Christian Martial Arts Ministry should be to avoid conflict as best we can. If we can de-escalate a situation verbally and negotiate the dynamics to a peaceful resolution conflict can often be avoided.

Many of us may view mixed martial arts competitions yet the Bible makes it very clear not to admire the man of violence. Some of you may question or challenge the notion that those practicing mixed martial arts and competing in these types of events would constitute violence. I would encourage you to look at this situation with open eyes - two men fighting, in a cage (like an animal) for 3 to 5 rounds.

The fundamental question here is; for what purpose are they fighting? In ancient times in Japan it was said that if one uses the self-preservation techniques taught for any other reason other than the defense of one's life, one's family, or one's Lord the techniques would utterly fail.

The basic principle behind this is that when you are fighting with love as the driving purpose you will be enabled to do what you may previously have thought impossible to do. From Scripture we know that all things are possible in God, and that all the law is fulfilled in this – love.

Make no mistake about it love has to be the compelling force that drives us into action when the time arises that we need to physically intervene. Do not underestimate this small but important detail – it is not about our egos, not about how well we have trained, and it surely not about operating out of pride or arrogance. Remember pride comes before fall.

Chapter 3: What is a Martial Arts Ministry

What is a Martial Arts Ministry? Well a lot of that depends on who you ask, and potentially when in history you ask it. Today's contemporary churches that have established Martial Arts Ministries may utilize their ministry for the youth or as a form of fellowship – all of which is great but I think it's important to reevaluate how we define a Martial Arts Ministry.

Although fellowship and youth engagement are desirable results of establishing a Martial Arts Ministry, it should not be the primary focus of a Martial Arts Ministry. The primary focus of a Martial Arts Ministry is to disciple believers in the faith while preparing them in a realistic way to overcome dangerous life threatening situations through the use of Martial Arts.

It should be noted here that although Martial Arts can be used as a tool that God uses to ultimately lead someone to the knowledge of the truth in Jesus Christ, evangelism is not the primary goal of a Martial Arts Ministry.

Now there's nothing wrong with doing public demonstrations of various skills that you may have acquired from the Martial Arts Ministry to help generate interest in learning more about your ministry. However, it should not be something that is regularly done. Consider doing these types of demonstrations once or twice a year at most.

And while we're discussing demonstrations, it's important to note here that demo teams that demonstrate various katas or set patterns and routines of weapons or hand-to-hand techniques is not something that you should be demonstrating because they provide little value to your overall goal.

In fact, in my humble opinion these set movements give the student a false sense of security and offer little in the way of practical self-defense techniques. These types of so-called martial arts styles actually make the students learning it less safe.

I know this may offend some of the traditional martial arts instructors out there who rely heavily on these types of set patterns and techniques but I'm hoping that you remain focus on what your purpose is as a Christian Martial Arts Instructor. Remember one of the primary goals of a Martial Arts Ministry is to prepare students to defend themselves in life-threatening situations in a realistic way – key word to remember here is, "Realistic".

Chapter 4: Why Start of Martial Arts Ministry

So why start a Martial Arts Ministry? Are you looking to add a new dynamic dimension to your church outreach, are looking for believers to exercise together, or maybe you just want to share your love of martial arts with your brothers and sisters in your church. While these answers may seem reasonable and logical - they are in fact bad answers.

You should only start a Martial Arts Ministry after praying to God regarding the matter. If God doesn't supernaturally drop within your heart a burden to start a Martial Arts Ministry you should not start one, as you will end up doing more harm than good going outside of the will of God.

You have to hear God speaking to your heart and giving you a vision that is unshakable. It is when God puts within your heart and your mind this desire then you can be assured that God is leading you down the path to start a Martial Arts Ministry. You can be assured that God will Bless you and your ministry if you're operating under these types of Biblical principles.

Now understand when you begin to move forward and start the process of creating a Martial Arts Ministry you will have opposition. Expect opposition to come from unexpected places such as your church leadership, if you are in fact affiliated with a church. Keep in mind that your spiritual enemy the devil will seek every opportunity that presents itself to destroy what God has called you to do. Therefore you must be ever vigilant, put on the full Armor of God, and walk up rightly before the Lord.

There is a higher level of expectations for Christian Martial Arts Instructors. You must conduct yourself in a manner that is above reproach. Not doing so is surely to cause problems and may in fact destroy your ministry. Lead by example followed by choice.

Like starting a new job, starting a Martial Arts Ministry has its ups and downs as you go through a learning process to master the basic skills necessary for your ministry to run smoothly. Keep in mind some of these basic skills are in fact spiritual skills such as spiritual warfare, understanding your enemy, and staying in the Word of God and prayed up. These skills may be self-evident to some but they're worth mentioning for those who haven't considered such things. One of the key principles is to press on and endure regardless of what the enemy may throw at you. What does Scripture say, "Stand strong in the Lord in the power of his might".

Chapter 5: Organizational Structure

Independent from Any and All Churches

Your organizational structure of your Martial Arts Ministry is critical to the Lord successfully utilizing your ministry to affect real change in believer's lives. This particular section should not be glanced over hastily but should be studied to gain a full grasp of the reality of what organizational structure is needed.

Once again this particular section may offend those with a religious spirit or those individuals with narrow minds. The things that I will discuss in this particular chapter are in fact factual and can be looked up with relative ease. I encourage everyone to do their own research and come to their own conclusions.

It's important to remember to, "Think for Yourself and Learn Directly from God" – AJF

If you cannot think for yourself then it's quite clear that you should not be starting a Martial Arts Ministry at this time. All Christian Martial Arts Instructors must, I repeat, must be able to think for themselves. The reason why stress this so much is because many 501c3 churches have dual loyalties to the government and to God.

However, we know from Scripture that no one can have two masters – you will end up loving one and hating the other. Scripture also makes it very clear that you cannot drink the cup of the Lord and the cup of demons. Most 501c3 churches have sold out to the government by merely accepting such a deal.

They exchange their silence on political issues or social issues for tax breaks – that's the simple reality. Again I encourage you to look up what churches can legally say or do once they become classified as a 501c3 entity.

As a result of this infiltration and depraved nature of the corporations that are classified as churches they preach a feel-good message to the congregation in hopes to attract more parishioners.

The reality is with a big expensive bill in the form of a mortgage or rent at a particular building church leaders often give feel-good messages instead of sound Biblical doctrine. We are warned in the last days that there will be doctrines of demons, false Christ, an increase of people having itchy ears.

The submission doctrine is one such doctrine the falls right in line with everything I previously mentioned. It's a combination of your 501c3 doctrine if you would as well as those doctrines of demons. Romans 13 is often quoted by government officials warning Christians to be good obedient serfs. Yet Romans 13 is not talking about a physical government, it is talking about a spiritual government.

Any church that preaches submission to the government as being obedience to God is teaching false doctrine. Your allegiance and your loyalty is always to the Kingdom of God and Christ not to your church, not to denomination, and surely not to any government.

Yet the submission doctrine is tame compared to what are known as Clergy Response Teams. Believe it or not my brothers and sisters pastors and leaders within your local church may in fact be literally on the payroll of the United States government. I know what you may be thinking at this particular point that can't be right, that must be a mistake, or some kind of conspiracy.

However unfortunate it is in fact a reality and I tell you the truth before God and do not lie. Once again I strongly encourage anyone that does not believe what I'm saying to investigated for themselves.

Your Martial Arts Ministry must remain fiercely independent from any and all influences from local churches, denominations, or political groups.

Does that mean we should not involve ourselves in politics? Absolutely not, what I'm referring to here is maintaining the integrity of your Martial Arts Ministry and not allowing it to be a pawn in the grand chess game. In fact it is our moral obligation and Christian duty to be involved in politics on a local level to speak out against the evils in our society whether they be corruption, abortion, or tyranny.

If you're a Christian Martial Arts Instructor in the United States of America it is important to uphold the rule of law that we go by in The Constitution of United States America.

Regardless of your geographical location, country of origin, native language, or racial background it's important to actively and passively promote Faith, Family, and Freedom to your students, your society, and of course the world at large via the Internet. Keep in mind just because you may be a small ministry that doesn't mean you can't have a big impact – God is Able.

Christian Martial Arts Instructors outside the United States of America face specific challenges to their particular region or country in the world. International Instructors should be mindful of different laws that may in fact make your Martial Arts Ministry illegal. You will in effect face the same challenges as the early disciples faced if this is the case.

However, the disciples made it clear we ought to obey God rather than man regardless of the consequence. Too many Christians nowadays, especially men are not bold in Christ - we have to reverse this trend as time is of the essence.

Other considerations for international Christian Martial Arts Instructors may be particular customs or norms specific to your location. There is no way for me to give you guidance on every particular location, only to refer you to the leading of the Holy Spirit. You and you alone know best what your situation is, if you are seeking answers than the best place to start is in prayer. God will no doubt guide you through His Holy Spirit if you commit your heart and your mind to serving Him completely and totally.

Given that Islam and sharia law are on the rise throughout the world and Christians have literally been targeted, drowned, and beheaded for their faith it is clear to see that Islam is not a religion of peace.

In fact Islam is not a religion in the purest sense, it masquerades as a religion to infiltrate a land and then establishes its dominance – it truly is a method and strategy of conquest.

As a Christian Martial Arts Instructor is imperative that you prepare your Christian students to defend themselves against those that practice Islam and wish to cut off their heads. I know this may sound extreme or even ridiculous to some, but make no mistake they are at war with Christians and Jews whether you want to accept that or not.

Remember Jesus warned us, "In the last days will be hated and all of the world for His namesake". We have to prepare our students to endure this – for the Scriptures declare, "He who endures till the end will be saved".

It's important to understand that those that practice Islam do not worship the same God as the Jews or Christians. Their doctrine came from a fallen angel, perhaps the devil himself. Acceptance or tolerance of Islam or sharia law is unacceptable for the Christian Martial Arts Instructor to teach. Nor any interfaith service that incorporates false doctrine like Islam.

Communist countries, dictatorships, and oppressive countries worldwide will have its own unique set of circumstances that present themselves. Remember no matter where your location you are to preach the gospel of the Kingdom of God. Part of that kingdom includes faith, family, and freedom. This will no doubt be contradictory to any such oppressive form of government.

Understand that these types of governments attempt to control the population in such a way where the state or the country becomes the people's God. This is especially true in communist countries such as Russia and China. And if you live in America it's important to understand that we are just as bad if not worse off, the only difference is the methods of control are more hidden and sophisticated.

No form of socialist, communist, or so-called democracy should be tolerated in any Martial Arts Ministry. These are doctrines of demons and should be weeded out before it infects your entire ministry. Some may see the word democracy and take issue that it is included here.

However, democracy is very simply mob rule or majority rule. Often times the story of two wolves and a sheep voting on what's for dinner is spoken of to describe a democracy. Democracy is no better than a monarchy, socialism, or the dreaded communist form of government. Keep that in mind as you move forward.

For those that are confused and assumed America was a democracy, it is not. It is in fact a representative republic. In a representative republic the rights of all are protected and that's the key thing – that in fact is an element of Christianity.

Missions, should your Martial Arts Ministry be involved in missions overseas and in other countries? I would encourage you to be led by the Spirit of God in this, but as a general rule of thumb I was so your mission should be local. You only have so many resources to draw from and if you are just starting out it's going to be even tougher.

Therefore I would recommend that you address the homeless, the needy, and the hungry in your local area before or in lieu of being involved in ministries around the world.

Now that's not to say if God has richly blessed you and has called you to help your brother or sister in a far-off land not to do that – by all means follow the leading of the Holy Spirit. These are just general guidelines and recommendations to focus your efforts and help enable you to be as successful as possible.

Should you or your Martial Arts Ministry join a Christian association, organization, or club? Or maybe you think you should apply to a secular organization or association to help validate or solidify in some way who and what you are to the world.

I would highly caution against this unless you have directly interacted with such organizations or associations previously. There are numerous types of these organizations out there ready and willing to take your money and give you whatever fancy title you desire.

If we look further and a little deeper into various Christian associations or organizations out there you have to ask yourself one question how will they benefit your Martial Arts Ministry?

I personally was involved with probably the largest Christian martial arts organization previously. I was even a state representative for Maryland and given a fancy rank within that organization's ranking body.

However, it became quite clear the more that I interacted with them that it was another instrument of control by those seeking to oppress the truth. Now keep in mind this organization did not address any political issues or rather any issues in the political arena at all – do we not have an obligation, yes a moral obligation in fact the stand in the gap when we see evil? Is this not one of the points of creating a Martial Arts Ministry?

Again look deep into whatever organization or association you may be considering joining. Most will talk the talk but won't walk the walk.

This is one of the reasons why the American Christian Defense Alliance exist. We started out as a Martial Arts Ministry as well as an organization to help guide those who have Christian Martial Arts Ministries. Yes, I know this is a bit of a shameless plug but honestly there's no other organization that I'm aware of here in the United States that does what we do – that takes a stand against the forces of darkness in real ways and helps encourage others to do the same, it just doesn't exist outside of our organization. Again I encourage you to do your own research and find out for yourself.

If you do create a Martial Arts Ministry and would like to join our organization we'd love to have you. For what does the Scriptures say, "The harvest is truly great but the workers are few". Just check out our website for the latest information and if you have any questions please email us.

As I mentioned previously you may be seeking to join an organization like ours for validation, ranking, or certifications.

We do provide these services to affiliate schools and certified instructors within our organization. However, if it's a question of being legitimate or not you have to stop looking at doing things the way that the world does them.

It is the Holy Spirit who certifies you and legitimizes you by giving you the wisdom and ability that only you have. You don't need a piece of paper stating you're an expert martial arts master or to create a Martial Arts Ministry if in fact you have genuine skills and abilities that the Lord has given you outside of "Traditional" means.

Look at the example of Christ and all the apostles. Ask yourself this question where did they study, where did they receive their certification and authority to teach to the people? Was it from the Rabbis, the Scribes, or the Pharisees? No, it came directly from God and through faith they move forward as the Holy Spirit gave them power and led them where God wanted. But it was that initial step of faith, it was that courage that led to confidence which enables them to proclaim boldly the Gospel of the Kingdom of God to the world around them.

So just understand certification, validation, and being legitimate comes from God, not man. As you walk in integrity you will know if you are legitimate or a liar.

That being said, I hope that I have helped clarify things better for you. Again we are always here is a resource to help guide you in your journey and hope that you will reach out to us as you move forward with faith and courage.

Chapter 6: Leadership Structure

Leadership structure in your Christian Martial Arts Ministry should include only men according to Scripture.

Let's look to the Scripture for clarification on this. Jesus, the 12 disciples, elders, and deacons all clearly leaders in the ministry in some way shape or form. As we can see all these positions have been or should be filled by men of God. In fact Jesus when He was choosing his 12 disciples chose all men (Mark 3:13-19).

According to the Word of God, women are to remain silent in churches, submit to their own husbands, and not have authority over men for this is what is good and acceptable before the Lord (1 Cor. 14:33-35, 1 Tim 2:11-12, Col. 3:18, 1 Peter 3:1-2).

In fact God ordained the husband to rule over their wife in Gen.3:16 after sin entered the world. We have to understand that there is a Biblical hierarchy, a natural order of things that God has established.

Eph. 5:22-24:

22 Wives, submit yourselves unto your own husbands, as unto the Lord. 23 For the husband is the head of the wife, even as Christ is the head of the church: and He is the saviour of the body.
24 Therefore as the church is subject unto Christ, so let the wives be to their own husbands in everything.

Understand you are effectively becoming the pastor of your Martial Arts Ministry. This comes with great responsibility and duty to teach and disciple accurately according to the Scriptures.

Take Heed to Your Duties Acts 20:25-32:

25 And now, behold, I know that ye all, among whom I have gone preaching the Kingdom of God, shall see my face no more. 26 Wherefore I take you to record this day, that I am pure from the blood of all men. 27 For I have not shunned to declare unto you all the counsel of God. 28 Take heed therefore unto yourselves, and to all the flock, over the which the Holy Ghost hath made you overseers, to feed the church of God, which he hath purchased with his own blood. 29 For I know this, that after my departing shall grievous wolves enter in among you, not sparing the flock.

30 Also of your own selves shall men arise, speaking perverse things, to draw away disciples after them.
31 Therefore watch, and remember, that by the space of three years I ceased not to warn every one night and day with tears. 32 And now, brethren, I commend you to God, and to the word of his grace, which is able to build you up, and to give you an inheritance among all them which are sanctified.

The American Christian Defense Alliance follows the Biblical example of having only men in leadership positions within the ministry. This is not to say that women cannot be in support roles but at no point in time should they be in leadership or teaching positions. If you are Christian Martial Arts Instructor and want to become an affiliate school you must be a man of God rightly dividing the Scriptures.

Chapter 7: Spiritual Structure

Having a mission statement and a vision statement typed nice and neatly isn't going to cut it. The Spiritual structure of your Martial Arts Ministry should go deep and be part of the foundation of your actual ministry. Part of the structure should include a statement of faith. Proclaiming and teaching proper doctrine is fundamental to successful discipleship.

Our Statement of Faith:

Let's looks at the Scriptures for Clarification:

And that from a child thou hast known the holy scriptures, which are able to make thee wise unto salvation through faith which is in Christ Jesus.

16All scripture is given by inspiration of God, and is profitable for doctrine, for reproof, for correction, for instruction in righteousness: 17That the man of God may be perfect, thoroughly furnished unto all good works. (2 Timothy 3:15-17)

We have also a more sure word of prophecy; whereunto ye do well that ye take heed, as unto a light that shineth in a dark place, until the day dawn, and the day star arise in your hearts: 20 Knowing this first, that no prophecy of the scripture is of any private interpretation. 21 For the prophecy came not in old time by the will of man: but holy men of God spake as they were moved by the Holy Ghost (2 Peter 1:19-21).

13 For this cause also we thank God without ceasing, because, when ye received the word of God which ye heard of us, ye received it not as the word of men, but as it is in truth, the word of God, which effectually worketh also in you that believe.(1 Thessalonians 2:13)

We accept no other documents, books, or "revelations" other than the Bible itself. Furthermore, we accept the 66 Books of the Bible alone, and nothing more or less. The Bible is the final authority and trustworthy for faith and practice." Creeds: "We understand the Apostles' creed and the Nicene creed as the sufficient statements of the Christian faith."

The One True God: The one true God has revealed himself as the eternally self-existent "I AM," the Creator of heaven and earth and the Redeemer of mankind. He has further revealed himself as embodying the principles of relationship and association as Father, Son, and Holy Spirit (Deuteronomy 6:4; Isaiah 43:10, 11; Matthew 28:19; Luke 3:22).

THE ADORABLE GODHEAD : (examples, Matthew 28:19; 2 Corinthians 13:14; John 14:16,17) (Luke 1:35; 1 Corinthians 1:24; Matthew 11:25-27; 28:19; 2 Corinthians 13:14; 1 John 1:3,4) (John 1:18; 15:26; 17:11,21; Zechariah 14:9) (John 5:17-30,32,37; 8:17,18).

God is three in one or a Trinity (Matthew 3:16-17, 28:19; John 14:16-17; 2 Corinthians 13:14; Acts 2:32-33, John 10:30, 17:11, 21; 1 Peter 1:2).

There is only one God (Isaiah 43:10; 44:6, 8; John 17:3; 1 Corinthians 8:5-6; Galatians 4:8-9).God is omniscient or "knows all things" (Acts 15:18; 1 John 3:20), God is omnipotent or "all powerful" (Psalm 115:3; Revelation 19:6), God is omnipresent or "present everywhere" (Jeremiah 23:23, 24; Psalm 139), God is Sovereign (Zechariah 9:14; 1 Timothy 6:15-16), God is Holy (1 Peter 1:15), God is just or "righteous" (Psalm 19:9, 116:5, 145:17; Jeremiah 12:1), God is love (1 John 4:8), God is true (Romans 3:4; John 14:6), God is Spirit (John 4:24), God is the Creator of everything that exists (Genesis 1:1; Isaiah 44:24), God is infinite and eternal. He has always been God (Psalm 90:2; Genesis 21:33; Acts 17:24), God is immutable. He does not change (James 1:17; Malachi 3:6; Isaiah 46:9-10)

Trinity: "There is only one God, the Creator of the universe, who has three 'persons' or aspects, and inseparable yet unique parts of the whole." "We teach that the one true God is the Father, and the Son, and the Holy Ghost, three distinct persons, but of one and the same divine essence, equal in power, equal in eternity, equal in majesty, because each person possesses the one divine essence."

Jesus Christ is God: (John 1:1, 14, 10:30-33, 20:28; Colossians 2:9; Philippians 2:5-8; Hebrews 1:8), Jesus became a man (Philippians 2:1-11), Jesus is fully God and fully man (Colossians 2:9; 1 Timothy 2:5; Hebrews 4:15; 2 Corinthians 5:21), Jesus was sinless (1 Peter 2:22; Hebrews 4:15),

Jesus is the only way to God the Father (John 14:6; Matthew 11:27; Luke 10:22), Jesus died for the sins of each and every person in the world (1 John 2:2; 2 Corinthians 5:14; 1 Peter 2:24), Jesus' death was a substitutionary sacrifice. He died and paid the price for our sins, so that we might live. (1 Peter 2:24; Matthew 20:28; Mark 10:45), Jesus resurrected from the dead in physical form (John 2:19-21), Those who accept Jesus Christ, after they die, will live for eternity with Him (John 11:25, 26; 2 Corinthians 5:6) Those who reject Jesus Christ, after they die, will go to hell forever (Revelation 20:11-15, 21:8) Jesus will return to the earth (Acts 1:11), Christians will be raised from the dead when Jesus returns (1 Thessalonians 4:14-17).

Nature of Christ: Christ "is the One Mediator, fully God, fully man, in whose Person is effected the reconciliation between God and man."

Resurrection of Christ: Jesus Christ "died, was buried, and after three days was resurrected by God.

Atonement (Purpose for Christ's Death): Christ truly suffered, was crucified, dead, and buried, to reconcile His Father to us, and to be a sacrifice, not only for the original sin, but also for actual sins of men" "Through Jesus' death and resurrection God triumphed over sin."

Holy Spirit: "The Holy Spirit, proceeding from the Father and the Son, is of one substance, majesty, and glory with the Father and the Son, very and eternal God." "The Holy Spirit is the Spirit of God, fully divine. He inspired holy men of old to write the Scriptures. Through revelation He enables men to understand truth. The Holy Spirit is God (Acts 5:3-4; 1 Corinthians 2:11-12; 2 Corinthians 13:14).

God's Law: The Law of God is "embodied in the Ten Commandments", which continue to be binding upon Christians. Furthermore, God has written His Law on our Hearts and no one needs to have anyone teach another, for it is the Spirit of God that will teach according to God's time not ours.

Man was created by God in the image of God (Genesis 1:26-27). Original Sin: "Man is very far gone from the original righteousness, and of his own nature inclined to evil, and that continually."

The Fall of Man: Man was created good and upright; for God said, "Let us make man in our image, after our likeness." However, man by voluntary transgression fell and thereby incurred not only physical death but also spiritual death, which is separation from God (Genesis 1:26, 27; 2:17; 3:6; Romans 5:12-19).

All people have sinned: (Romans 3:23, 5:12), Death came into the world through Adam's sin (Romans 5:12-15), Sin separates us from God (Isaiah 59:2),

Free Will: "Man is truly free only when he is in communion and harmony with God's Word; otherwise he is only a slave to his body or to the world. At the Fall, "man's will became blurred, but did not disappear." "We have no power to do good works, pleasant and acceptable to God, without the grace of God working through us by the power of the Holy Spirit."

Body and Soul: "The unity of soul and body is so profound that one has to consider the soul to be the "form" of the body; spirit and matter, in man, not two natures united, but rather their union forms a single nature.

Material and spiritual realities are "closely bound together. Human life and human fulfillment are inextricably bound to both the physical and the spiritual dimensions of human existence."

The Human Condition: Human Beings are by nature evil, sinful, and deceitful. Roman 3:9-18 says, [9] What then? Are we better than they? No, in no wise: for we have before proved both Jews and Gentiles, that they are all under sin; [10] As it is written, There is none righteous, no, not one: [11] There is none that understandeth, there is none that seeketh after God. [12] They are all gone out of the way, they are together become unprofitable; there is none that doeth good, no, not one.

[13] Their throat is an open sepulchre; with their tongues they have used deceit; the poison of asps is under their lips: [14] Whose mouth is full of cursing and bitterness: [15] Their feet are swift to shed blood: [16] Destruction and misery are in their ways: [17] And the way of peace have they not known: [18] There is no fear of God before their eyes. [19] Now we know that what things soever the law saith, it saith to them who are under the law: that every mouth may be stopped, and all the world may become guilty before God. Furthermore, Romans 3:23 states, "For all have sinned, and come short of the glory of God;"

Grace: Ephesians 2:8-9 States, "For by grace are ye saved through faith; and that not of yourselves: it is the gift of God: Not of works, lest any man should boast".

Salvation is a free gift of God.

If we say that we have no sin, we deceive ourselves, and the truth is not in us. If we confess our sins, he is faithful and just to forgive us our sins, and to cleanse us from all unrighteousness (1 John 1:8-10) (Romans 4:5, 6:23).

Salvation: "Salvation involves the redemption of the whole man, and is offered freely to all who accept Jesus Christ as Lord and Savior." "We are accounted righteous before God, only because of the blood that was shed for each of us, granting us grace and by living a life of faith through the power of the Holy Spirit."

"The acceptance of Christ as the Savior through confession in Christ as the True God is the highest gift given to the believer by the Holy Spirit. ...acceptance is his own choice through his own free will. This is why one is responsible for his own fate."

The Salvation of Man: Man's only hope of redemption is through the shed blood of Jesus Christ the Son of God. Conditions to Salvation: Salvation is received through repentance toward God and faith toward the Lord Jesus Christ.

By the washing of regeneration and renewing of the Holy Spirit, being justified by grace through faith, man becomes an heir of God according to the hope of eternal life (Luke 24:47; John 3:3; Romans 10:13-15; Ephesians 2:8; Titus 2:11; 3:5-7). The Evidences of Salvation: The inward evidence of salvation is the direct witness of the Spirit (Romans 8:16). The outward evidence to all men is a life of righteousness and true holiness (Ephesians 4:24; Titus 2:12).

Preservation of Salvation: You can lose your Salvation!!! Possible to lose salvation if fall into sin without repentance

Purgatory: Denied

Predestination: Many are Called, but few are Chosen. There are vessels for honor and vessels for dishonor. "Predestination to Life is the everlasting purpose of God... to deliver from curse and damnation those whom he hath chosen in Christ out of mankind, and to bring them by Christ to everlasting salvation, as vessels made to honor."

Sanctification: Sanctification is an act of separation from that which is evil, and of dedication unto God (Romans 12:1, 2; 1 Thessalonians 5:23; Hebrews 13:12). Scriptures teach a life of "holiness without which no man shall see the Lord" (Hebrews 12:14). By the power of the Holy Spirit we are able to obey the command: "Be ye holy, for I am holy" (1 Peter 1:15, 16).

Sanctification is realized in the believer by recognizing his identification with Christ in His death and resurrection, and by faith reckoning daily upon the fact of that union, and by offering every faculty continually to the dominion of the Holy Spirit (Romans 6:1-11,13; 8:1,2,13; Galatians 2:20; Philippians 2:12,13; 1 Peter 1:5).

Good Works: Is a direct result of your faith. Faith without works is dead. "Although good works, which are the fruits of faith, and follow after justification, cannot put away our sins, and endure the severity of God's judgment; yet they are pleasing and acceptable to God in Christ, and spring out of a true and lively faith." "Those who truly have faith in Christ live out that faith, expressing compassion for others for whom He died."

Prayer: Is talking to God. It helps to sanctify things (1 Tim 4:5), Prayer heals people and removes sin (James 5:15-16), We are also to pray without ceasing always (Eph. 1:16, 6:18). When you pray – You are to believe you will receive (Matt. 21:22) The 9th hour of the day is the hour of Pray according to Scripture (Acts 3:1)

The Baptism in the Holy Spirit: Will naturally occur as a result of your faith. Believers do not need to actively seek out being Baptized in the Holy Spirit. Being baptized in the Holy Spirit was the normal experience of all in the early Christian church. With it comes the endowment of power for life and service, the bestowment of the gifts and their uses in the work of the ministry (Luke 24:49; Acts 1:4, 8; 1 Corinthians 12:1-31).

This experience is distinct from and subsequent to the experience of the new birth (Acts 8:12-17; 10:44-46; 11:14-16; 15:7-9). With the baptism in the Holy Spirit come such experiences as an overflowing fullness of the Spirit (John 7:37-39; Acts 4:8), a deepened reverence for God (Acts 2:43; Hebrews 12:28), an intensified consecration to God and dedication to His work (Acts 2:42), and a more active love for Christ, for His Word, and for the lost (Mark 16:20).

Sabbath: We believe God's Word does not change, God has commanded that we "Honor the Sabbath" and use it for a day of rest and we shall. Sabbath is an important part of the belief and practice of this organization. The Sabbath should be observed on the seventh day of the week, specifically, from Friday sunset to Saturday sunset.

Believers should observe Sabbath on the seventh Hebrew day of the week, from Friday sunset to Saturday sunset, in similar manner as in Judaism, rather than on Sunday like a larger segment of Christianity. We believe that keeping seventh-day Sabbath weekly and physically is a moral responsibility, equal to that of any other of the Ten Commandments, that honors God as Creator and Deliverer. The requirement to keep the seventh day holy is found in the fourth commandment of God's Law in the book of Exodus.

Sabbath activities: Much of Friday might be spent in preparation for the Sabbath; for example, preparing meals and tidying homes. Some members gather for Friday evening worship to welcome in the Sabbath, a practice often known as Vespers. To keep the weekly Sabbath holy, members abstain from secular work on Saturday. They will also usually refrain from purely secular forms of recreation, such as competitive sport and watching non-religious programs on television.

However, nature walks, family-oriented activities, charitable work and other activities that are compassionate in nature are encouraged. Saturday afternoon activities vary widely depending on the cultural, ethnic and social background. In some churches, members and visitors will participate in a fellowship (or "potluck") lunch

The Ordinances of the Church:

Baptism in Water: The ordinance of baptism by immersion is commanded in the Scriptures. All who repent and believe on Christ as Savior and Lord are to be baptized. Thus they declare to the world that they have died with Christ and that they also have been raised with Him to walk in newness of life (Matthew 28:19; Mark 16:16; Acts 10:47, 48; Romans 6:4).

Communion: This means an actual meal consisting of the same elements (bread and wine) that the disciples ate with Jesus. It is a symbol expressing our sharing the divine nature of our Lord Jesus Christ (2 Peter 1:4); a memorial of His suffering and death (1 Corinthians 11:26); and a prophecy of His second coming (1 Corinthians 11:26); and is enjoined on all believers "till He come!"

The Ministry: A divinely called and scripturally ordained ministry has been provided by our Lord for the fourfold purpose of leading the Church in: (1) Discipleship of the world (Mark 16:15-20), (2) worship of God (John 4:23,24), (3) building a Body of saints being perfected in the image of His Son (Ephesians 4:11,16), and (4) Meeting human needs with ministries of love and compassion (Psalms 112:9; Galatians 2:10; 6:10; James 1:27).

Obligations as a part of God's Remnant: Do not partake in the things of this world that are contrary to the Nature and Word of God. We are to be in the world but not of this world as a testimony to those around us. All believers are encouraged to understand and remember that heaven and earth will pass away but His Word will remain the same.

Society is always changing, most of the times not for the good of mankind, yet throughout societies God's Word will remain constant and continue to be the Standard for All believers regardless of Country, Culture, or Society. It is up to us as believers in the faith to walk out our faith with fear and trembling before God despite the consequences or repercussions of those around us.

Remember, the ruler of this world is Satan, our spiritual enemy, and he continues to walk to and fro like a roaring lion seeking whom he can devour. He comes only to Lie, Kill, and Destroy. Therefore, we ought to obey God Rather than Man!

No Celebration of Pagan "Holidays" such as Christmas, Easter, Halloween, etc. As believers in the faith we must understand that Christ did not come to destroy the law, but to fulfill it. If we take Jesus Christ as our example on how to follow you can see that even Jesus honored the Sacred Holy Days such as Passover that God has set in place. We also must remember and honor these sacred holy days God has set apart, but in a Christian way that will differ from those practicing Judaism.

Respect Life and the Potential of Every Human Being: As long as there is breath in our lungs there is Hope - Hope in God for a better future. Furthermore, even after breath fleas from our lungs there is yet hope in a real and powerful God as we can see in the ministry of Jesus raising Lazarus from the dead and even from God Himself when He raised Jesus up from the dead.

Having stated the above we do not believe in abortion, suicide, euthanasia, birth control (for married couples), blood transfusions or the giving of blood in any way (Hebrews 9: 13 – 10:4), cloning, genetically modified organisms (GMOs), Body Piercing for Men (acceptable for women in ears only),

We feel that tattoos are a personal decision and are acceptable permitting they should forth the Glory of God and are a representation of your personal testimony. However, tattoos to the face, neck, and other areas not suitable for blending into the general population to the point it would hinder finding gainful employment is not encouraged.

Furthermore, we believe in honoring the Temple of the Living God, i.e. your body by not smoking, or using any drugs. One should remain guarded with possibilities to become addicted to anything and always seek to honor God by honoring your body, and that of your families.

Oaths, Pacts and Covenants: Let your yes be yes and you no be no. Furthermore, do not say that you will do this or that but say if the Lord wills you will do this or that.

Family integrated worship: We reject the idea of Saturday/Sunday School, viewing it as unscriptural and interfering with the right of parents to give religious instruction to their children. Instead, children are expected to attend at least part of the church service.

Informal training of preachers: The American Christian Defense Alliance rejects theological seminaries they have "no warrant or sanction from the New Testament, nor in the example of Christ and the apostles."

Divine Healing: Divine healing is an integral part of the gospel. Deliverance from sickness is provided for in the Atonement, and is the privilege of all believers (Isaiah 53:4, 5; Matthew 8:16, 17; James 5:14-16).

Anointing with Oil and Laying on of the Hands: There is no example found in the Bible where women lay hands on anyone.

Therefore, Men are to lay hands on other Men only, especially in a corporate gathering. Husbands are to lay hands on their wife, and children as necessary in private but should never lay hands on any other female or child unless consent is expressed by the father of that child. Women are forbidden to lay hands on anyone outside of their home and should only be done in the absence and with the blessing of the Husband and Father.

Global Government: The American Christian Defense Alliance is against any form of global government, global banks, and centralized global religions. We find the beauty in the distinctiveness of sovereign countries and their traditions. However, we understand that in the last days these things will occur.

New World Order and a Global Conspiracy: Ez. 22:23-31, Ps. 2

Ez. 22:23-31 - [23] And the word of the Lord came unto me, saying, [24] Son of man, say unto her, Thou art the land that is not cleansed, nor rained upon in the day of indignation. [25] There is a conspiracy of her prophets in the midst thereof, like a roaring lion ravening the prey; they have devoured souls; they have taken the treasure and precious things; they have made her many widows in the midst thereof. [26] Her priests have violated my law, and have profaned mine holy things: they have put no difference between the holy and profane, neither have they shewed difference between the unclean and the clean, and have hid their eyes from my Sabbaths, and I am profaned among them. [27] Her princes in the midst thereof are like wolves ravening the prey, to shed blood, and to destroy souls, to get dishonest gain.

^{28} And her prophets have daubed them with untempered morter, seeing vanity, and divining lies unto them, saying, Thus saith the Lord God, when the Lord hath not spoken. ^{29} The people of the land have used oppression, and exercised robbery, and have vexed the poor and needy: yea, they have oppressed the stranger wrongfully. ^{30} And I sought for a man among them, that should make up the hedge, and stand in the gap before me for the land, that I should not destroy it: but I found none. ^{31} Therefore have I poured out mine indignation upon them; I have consumed them with the fire of my wrath: their own way have I recompensed upon their heads, saith the Lord God.

Psalm 2:

Why do the heathen rage, and the people imagine a vain thing? 2 The kings of the earth set themselves, and the rulers take counsel together, against the Lord, and against his anointed, saying,

3 Let us break their bands asunder, and cast away their cords from us. 4 He that sitteth in the heavens shall laugh: the Lord shall have them in derision. 5 Then shall he speak unto them in his wrath, and vex them in his sore displeasure. 6 Yet have I set my king upon my holy hill of Zion. 7 I will declare the decree: the Lord hath said unto me, Thou art my Son; this day have I begotten thee. 8 Ask of me, and I shall give thee the heathen for thine inheritance, and the uttermost parts of the earth for thy possession.

⁹ Thou shalt break them with a rod of iron; thou shalt dash them in pieces like a potter's vessel. ¹⁰ Be wise now therefore, O ye kings: be instructed, ye judges of the earth. ¹¹ Serve the Lord with fear, and rejoice with trembling.
¹² Kiss the Son, lest he be angry, and ye perish from the way, when his wrath is kindled but a little. Blessed are all they that put their trust in him.

Angels:
Ps. 104:3-5 - Angels are also spirits
Gen. 28:12 - Angels ascend and descend from heaven
Ps. 78:24-26 - Angels eat manna in the corn of heaven
Matt. 22:29-31 - Angels don't marry, nor are they given in marriage
Ps. 78:48-50 - God still commands evil or fallen Angels
Matt. 4:11 - God sends angels to minister to us
Mat. 18:10 - Angels are assigned to watch over children

Ps. 91:11 - God sends angels to keep us on the straight and narrow
Matt. 22:29-31 - We become like the Angels after the resurrections
Matt. 13:39 - The reapers of the harvest are the Angels
Matt. 16:27 - Holy Angels will come back with Jesus
Matt. 13:41 / 13:49 Jesus will send his Holy angels to gather out all things that offend and to do iniquity – they shall sever the wicked from the just

Rev. 12:9 - In the last days the devil and his angels are kicked out of heaven and cast down to earth
Matt. 25:41 - The devil and his angels are cursed by God and cast into everlasting fire.

False Doctrine: 1 Tim 4:1-2 - Now the Spirit speaketh expressly, that in the latter times some shall depart from the faith, giving heed to seducing spirits, and doctrines of devils; [2] Speaking lies in hypocrisy; having their conscience seared with a hot iron;

Matthew 24:4-5, 9-13

[4] And Jesus answered and said unto them, Take heed that no man deceive you. [5] For many shall come in my name, saying, I am Christ; and shall deceive many. . . . [9] Then shall they deliver you up to be afflicted, and shall kill you: and ye shall be hated of all nations for my name's sake.

[10] And then shall many be offended, and shall betray one another, and shall hate one another. [11] And many false prophets shall rise, and shall deceive many. [12] And because iniquity shall abound, the love of many shall wax cold. [13] But he that shall endure unto the end, the same shall be saved.

Mary the Mother of Jesus: Mary should not be regarded as a mediator between man and God, but she should be honored as the mother of "Jesus and a model for Christian women.

Demons and Satan: Demons are fallen angels who can never repent. Satan is a fallen Angel with great evil power and the current ruler of this world, but limited by God's providence.

Eternal Hell: Everlasting misery and separation from God is the final dwelling of those who neglect God's great salvation Hell is a place of punishment (Matthew 25:41, 46; Revelation 19:20), Hell is eternal (Matthew 25:46).

End Times / Last Days: The Saints of God will go through the Seals of God and after that be raptured. We have a Post-Tribulation doctrine

There will be a rapture of the church (Matthew 24:30-36, 40-41; John 14:1-3; 1 Corinthians 15:51-52; 1Thessalonians 4:16-17; 2 Thessalonians 2:1-12).

The Blessed Hope: The resurrection of those who have fallen asleep in Christ and their translation together with those who are alive and remain unto the coming of the Lord is the imminent and blessed hope of the Church (1Thessalonians 4:16,17; Romans 8:23; Titus 2:13; 1 Corinthians 15:51, 52).

The Millennial Reign of Christ: The second coming of Christ includes the rapture of the saints, which is our blessed hope, followed by the return of Christ with His saints to reign on the earth for one thousand years (Zechariah 14:5; Matthew 24:27,30; Revelation 1:7; 19:11-14; 20:1-6). This millennial reign will bring the salvation of national Israel (Ezekiel 37:21, 22; Zephaniah 3:19, 20; Romans 11:26, 27) and the establishment of universal peace (Isaiah 11:6-9; Psalm 72:3-8; Micah 4:3, 4).

There will be a final judgment (Hebrews 9:27; 2 Peter 3:7).

The Final Judgment: There will be a final judgment in which the wicked dead will be raised and judged according to their works. Whosoever is not found written in the Book of Life, together with the devil and his angels, the beast and the false prophet, will be consigned to everlasting punishment in the lake which burn with fire and brimstone, which is the second death (Matthew 25:46; Mark 9:43-48; Revelation 19:20; 20:11-15; 21:8). Satan will be thrown into the lake of fire (Revelation 20:10).

The New Heavens and the New Earth: "We, according to His promise, look for new heavens and a new earth, wherein dwell righteousness" (2 Peter 3:13; Revelation 21:1)

Heaven: There are 3 Heavens. The Firmament or Sky, The Universe, and the place the God dwells – where the Holy City is. Rev. 21:10-27 describes the Holy City.

Government Involvement:

Clergy Response Teams: We do not partake in any way in such activities for you cannot serve two masters – you will end up loving one and hating the other.

No Military Service: The concept we hold to is one of non-interventionist as The Constitution of the United States dictates. Furthermore, we hold to the concept of community and civil defense, understanding that it should be the force continuum that will dictate the response in any armed conflict.

With that being said, we do not advocate joining the military or being part of the military industrial complex in any way, nor do we encourage members to dishonor their bodies by allowing for testing of any kind from any agency; yet we do support those brave men who courageously wish to serve their communities directly and join the police force.

It is the believe of the American Christian Defense Alliance that only men should be the direct primary defenders in any conflict and that women should play a support roll limited to what is absolutely necessary. The American Christian Defense Alliance does support the concept of the "Black Regiment" and is actively seeking to develop one.

2nd Amendment: Firearms, one of the most controversial subjects here in America yet number two in the original Bill of Rights. The American Christian Defense Alliance, Inc. believes very strongly in the right of the people to keep and bare arms to protect themselves and their love ones.

The American Christian Defense Alliance, Inc. believes that firearms of any kind are merely a tool to ensure that liberty is past down to future generations and rejects the statement that, "Guns Kill People" in full. Firearms can do nothing in and of themselves, it is the person behind the operation of the firearm that is fully responsible for any and all actions in which may cause injury of some kind. Remember this:

Every time a nation has enacted a law to make firearms illegal great tyranny has risen up – From Nazi Germany, to the Communist Chinese all dictators would agree gun control works. When gun control works massive amounts of people are murdered by the state.

Professor John Lott has two good books about gun ownership and crime. Both of his books indicate that where there is more gun control there is more crime. Don't let it happen again here in America. I urge all of you reading this to get prepared asap because the time is coming and now is when this nation will seek to take away our 2nd Amendment Right to keep and bear arms.

As you can see developing sound doctrine and meticulously going through the word of God is not an easy thing but once you have sound doctrine written down, then what? How will you convey this information to your students and make believers into disciples?

It would be great if there was some kind of Bible study specifically designed for Christian Martial Arts students to use as they go throughout their belts. However, at this particular time there is no standardize Martial Arts Ministry Bible study curriculum because each ministry seems to be doing their own thing.

In an attempt to help standardize the education of the Christian Martial Arts Student within the American Christian Defense Alliance we have developed and published a book called, Bible Studies for Belts". Yes, I know, another shameless plug yet this information could save a tremendous time, energy, and effort when first starting out.

Part of our curriculum also involves teaching a servant's heart at the training Hall or dojo that transcends into the community. We do this by requiring a certain level of community service whether at the training Hall, dojo, or at your local homeless shelters, soup kitchens, or just out there on the streets. This particular aspect of our curriculum may open the eyes of those that are unaware of the destitute situations in our local communities. Through this awareness compassion springs forth into action and thus creates the servant's heart.

In the United States Street Preaching is also required as part of our curriculum. This may not be possible in your location but do your best to mirror what we are doing without compromising your situation. It is at our black belt level that we require Street Preaching against such things as abortions, sodomy, or any other evil of the day. Through this part of our curriculum we hope to establish a strong sense of faith, courage, and confidence that brings forth boldness.

Too often the so-called church has sat on the sidelines of the game of life. Too often those within church buildings refused to step outside of their comfort zones and address the murder of innocent life in the silent Holocaust we call abortion. We have to stand in the gap at every level – spiritually, physically, and eternally by being ever vigilant in guarding against the wolves that seek to destroy the flock.

If you're not standing in the gap, if you not standing up for Jesus you're falling for the devil and his lies – for faith without works is dead.

Chapter 8: Principles, Purpose, and Objectives

When seeking to develop a martial arts ministry it's important to remember some basic principles, objectives, and the true purpose for establishing a Martial Arts Ministry.

Some Principles, Purposes, and Objectives include the Following:

1. Draw Closer to God
2. Discipleship (Not Evangelism)
3. Build the Next Generation of Christian Leaders
4. To Save a Lives in Dangerous Situations
5. To Understand ONE man can Make a Difference (especially filled with the Spirit of God)
6. Stand Against what God hates according to His Word

Chapter 9: Where to Teach

So now that you've got some of the fundamental principles and structure out of the way where do you teach? As I previously mentioned I would be careful teaching at your church as inevitably there will be strings attached and you will not end up having full control over what's said and done in the ministry that God has called you to develop. It is your responsibility, yes your duty even to ensure that you remain in control of the ministry that God has called you to create. It needs to be God's Word coming through you loud and clear to the students He has entrusted you with.

You may be able to teach at a local community center, government school, or a strip mall. However, is that the best option when you're first starting out? Again you have to think about your funding, and the sources of your funding – where will they come from?

For the majority of Christian Martial Arts Instructors seeking to develop a Martial Arts Ministry such things as a strip mall, government school, or community centers are not realistic options – yet if you know someone or God opens up a door by all means take it.

Another option, especially for home churches is to utilize a shed or small building at your house. This is a great option when you're just starting out and don't have a lot of students as it protects you from the elements and is quite convenient. Yet one drawback from this type of situation involves the lack of boundaries in relationship to your students. For this reason alone I would not recommend this option.

The option that we have utilized, and continue to utilize is meeting at local parks to train. Not only is this a means of outreach but it's also a living testimony seen by those outside of church buildings.

Local parks offer a lot of advantages when training. Often times they will have restroom facilities available to the general public, picnic benches for family members not participating, and ample room to move around and train in a realistic way. Some parks even have pavilions that offer some protection from rain or excessive sun – if you can find those, without the picnic benches and chairs you found a great place to train.

Additionally the added benefits of fellowship after training are numerous. This is truly a great way to build a successful Martial Arts Ministry.

Chapter 10: How Much

As a Christian Martial Arts Instructor you may be wondering if you should charge at all, after all it is a ministry. However, every ministry needs funding to continue to provide services to those that they serve. Let's look to the Scriptures, what do the Scriptures say?

1 Cor. 9:9 ˙For it is written in the Law of Moses, thou shalt not muzzle the mouth of the ox that treadeth out the corn. Doth God take care for oxen?

1 Tim 5:18 -For the scripture saith, thou shalt not muzzle the ox that treadeth out the corn. And, The labourer is worthy of his reward.

What does Jesus think about charging? Well when He sent out the seventy in pairs what did He say?

Luke 10: 1-11

After these things the Lord
appointed other seventy also, and
sent them two and two before his
face into every city and place,
whither he himself would come.
² Therefore said he unto them, The
harvest truly is great, but the
labourers are few: pray ye therefore
the Lord of the harvest, that He
would send forth labourers into his
harvest *³ Go your ways: behold, I*
send you forth as lambs among
wolves. ⁴ Carry neither purse, nor
scrip, nor shoes: and salute no man
by the way. ⁵ And into whatsoever
house ye enter, first say, Peace be to
this house. ⁶ And if the son of peace
be there, your peace shall rest upon
it: if not, it shall turn to you again.
⁷ And in the same house remain,
eating and drinking such things as
they give: for the labourer is worthy
of his hire. Go not from house to
house. ⁸ And into whatsoever city ye
enter, and they receive you, eat such
things as are set before you:

⁹ And heal the sick that are therein, and say unto them, The kingdom of God is come nigh unto you. ¹⁰ But into whatsoever city ye enter, and they receive you not, go your ways out into the streets of the same, and say, ¹¹ Even the very dust of your city, which cleaveth on us, we do wipe off against you: otwithstanding be ye sure of this, that the kingdom of God is come nigh unto you.

So as we can see Jesus himself proclaims that the laborer is worthy of his wages. Understand brothers that you are part of the laborers for this great harvest and you must have the resources necessary for basic needs to be provided in your ministry to be successful.

As some of you may not wish to charge and that's perfectly fine but you need to seriously consider how your ministry to be funded.

If you do not want to charge money maybe you could develop a barter system that works for you and your students – just think outside of the box.

If you are going to charge then I would recommend charging between $20.00 and $60.00 a month per family. As a general rule of thumb I would not charge more than a half a day's wages per month. Now you may be asking what is an average day's pay, and for who a doctor, a lawyer, or a teacher. The second strategy can be employed regardless of geographic location or country and will be specifically tied to the economics of your location. Thus it is ideal for international implementation of a Christian Martial Arts Ministry.

With the price established you should also develop a special needs program for the poor and destitute of your location.

Chapter 11: Terminology

This may be one of the most overlooked concepts to consider when starting a Martial Arts Ministry. As a Christian Martial Arts Instructor you may have spent years perfecting your specific style. Along with that you gain years of experience, including proper terminology for your given martial arts style.

While this knowledge and experience has benefited you in the advancement of your particular art or style, it has little practical value when it comes to actually protecting human life. Remember brothers our focus needs to remain sharp, we must remain vigilant and not get hung up on useless terminology that acts to divide and not unite.

If our fundamental goal is to help enable the protection of human life it's critical that you speak your native language with your students during class.

Don't use complicated terminology in your class, stick to the national language of your country and keep things simple.

Another reason for this methodology is to limit the barriers to learning actual life-saving techniques. Your students shouldn't have to take college courses to learn Japanese, Chinese, or Korean languages just to comprehend what you're attempting to teach them. Communicate the techniques in a down to earth way at their level.

While were discussing communication here I think it's important to address what version of the Bible you will be using, such as the King James Version – and then stick to it. Being in one accord is a challenge but it can be done with the right heart.

Chapter 12: The Temple

Have you thought about developing a health and fitness program to complement your self-defense training? If you haven't thought too much about developing at least a nutritional plan to ensure you students get the best possible benefit from your Martial Arts Ministry you should consider it.

The Scripture is clear, Gen. 1:27 says "So God created man in His own image, in the image of God created Him, male and female, He created them."

We were given bodies as gift from God. The Bible tells us that our bodies is the temple of the Holy Spirit and that we should glorify and honor God through it (1 Cor. 6:19-20).

Yet, what's disappointing is that many people, even instructors do not take care of their bodies—they allow themselves to become unhealthy, consume junk food, binge eat, drink alcohol excessively, smoke cigarettes, abuse drugs, and commit other immoralities. These things should not be Brothers.

What most people don't realize is that the Spirit is also affected when we don't take care of our bodies.

The apostle Paul said in the letters to the Romans (12:1) "I beseech you therefore, brethren, by the mercies of God, that ye present your bodies a living sacrifice, holy, acceptable, unto God, which is your reasonable service."

If you were to present your body as a sacrifice to God, would you think that it would be acceptable before Him? What about your students?

If you think you need to improve on your lifestyle and start seeking ways to become healthy in order to present a more pleasing sacrifice to God, then guess what? God has even prescribed foods that are healthy and is good for our body—and these are fruits and vegetables.

"And God said, Behold, I have given you every herb bearing seed, which is upon the face of all the earth, and every tree, in the which is the fruit of a tree yielding seed; to you it shall be for meat...And the Lord God commanded the man, saying, of every tree of the garden thou mayest freely eat." Genesis 1:29 and Genesis 2:16.

I highly recommend that you include juicing in your plans. I will not lay out a specific plan here, as doing so would not cover every situation or set of dynamics for specific individuals. Health, Fitness, and Nutrition should be individualized for each student.

Chapter 13: What Style

Your development of a Martial Arts Ministry should be driven by a desire to serve the Lord and preserve life. That being said it's important to understand that a Martial Arts Ministry should have at its base a realistic style of Martial Arts to adequately preserve and protect life during those critical times when lives hang in the balance.

A true Martial Arts Ministry will incorporate a self-defense system that teaches actual lifesaving skills. In my humble opinion any martial art that is not reality-based and teaching a combat style of Martial Art can never truly be a Martial Arts Ministry.

For if the essence of a Martial Arts Ministry is to promote and to protect life at every turn, systems and styles that are not reality base leaves students with a false sense of security and puts them in even greater danger - thus negating a fundamental principle of a Martial Arts Ministry, to protect and to promote life.

If you are doing forms are caught us, or any set patterns you're wasting peoples time and setting them up for failure – you will be held accountable for that before God Almighty.

Realistic training for real-world – no competition, demo teams, or unrealistic training methods should be permitted.

Chapter 14: How Often To Hold Class

When you just starting your Martial Arts Ministry it's important to start off relatively slow depending upon what the Lord has instructed you to do. I recommend holding one class per week. This will help solidify your base students as well as create a buzz regarding your Martial Arts Ministry. After the word gets out you may want to increase how often you hold classes.

However, unless you are a full-time Martial Arts Ministry (meaning you own and operate a traditional dojo training hall) I would limit your classes to three days a week at the most. This type of structure will help to alleviate normal daily logistical concerns on the part of your students and increase your attendance. After all what good is holding class if no one shows up? Remember, no training on the Sabbath.

Chapter 15: What's The Best Day and Time

One of the main things you want to try to avoid is making things more difficult for your students to attend class regularly. Number one goal for choosing a day and time is to pick the best possible day to make it more probable for your students to attend. With this guiding principle we can narrow things down.

One important thing to remember is that you are going to want to avoid teaching from Friday at sunset to Saturday at sunset – this is the Sabbath. If you're going to start a Christian Martial Arts Ministry it's important that you understand fundamental things such as when the Sabbath is. This should not be overlooked or taken lightly – God said it for a reason.

So what's the Best Day and Time? Most likely other Christians will be in church on Sundays, therefore, it's a good idea to hold your class after the morning service but before the evening service. Allow time to possibly go home, take a shower and change before potentially returning for the evening service.

This will vary depending on denomination or belief but it's good to schedule things in a way people can fit it in to their daily lives. If you're doing it on a week day make sure its after normal work hours, say around 7pm. Try to make your class at least 2 hours long as well.

Chapter 16: Operational Structure

The operational structure of your martial arts ministry should include the development of a student handbook which includes fundamental things pertinent specifically to your martial arts ministry. If you join the American Christian Defense Alliance as an affiliate school we do have a student handbook available on Amazon for you to purchase.

One important thing to remember regarding your operational structure is how to properly interact with your students. You never want to put yourself in a compromising situation, or situation that could be considered inappropriate. Always conduct yourself in a manner that is above reproach in everything that you do.

One of the most important things that I cannot overstress is never to be alone with any student, especially one of the opposite sex. Allegations alone have ruined many ministries, again keep it above reproach and don't give room for the devil - for we know that he walks around like a roaring lion seeking whom he may devour. Keep the full armor of God on and take up the Sword of the Spirit – be vigilant, again I say be vigilant in everything that you do.

If you do not wish to join the American Christian Defense Alliance as an affiliate school and utilize our student handbook than it's important to at least come up with some basic parameters of your operational structure including the following:

- Rules of the class
- Uniforms
- Testing

Chapter 17: Get the Word Out About Your Ministry

Once you have your foundation down it's time to get the word out regarding your Martial Arts Ministry. Some of the best ways to get the word out include the following:

- Create a Simple Website with a few pages
- Create a You Tube page, Facebook Page, Twitter Account
- Email your friends, family, and church about the new Ministry
- Flyer and Brochures are also great - but you have to walk and get them out to everyone

Once you start the process of getting the word out and giving people your website address and social media account information it's important to keep your social media accounts updated.

Chapter 18: Your Impact on the World

Your impact on the world is unknown at this time – it will only be known in the end. Therefore it's important to give your all in everything that you do - have the understanding and faith that God is Able despite situations or circumstances that may be presently before you.

The Internet is an amazing tool that we can utilize for the Glory of God and the uplifting of His Kingdom. What once took several people and huge amounts of money to accomplish can now be accomplished with very little resources. There's a saying where I'm from, "Go big or go home". This basically means that you need to think big or not even try, it's very similar to when God says that He desires us to be hot or cold but not lukewarm.

So I encourage you today to be on fire for God and give all you got until there's nothing left to give.

As a Christian Martial Arts Instructor it's important to extend your reach with the use of social media as well as developing a website. This will help increase your potential impact on the world. Much like a weapon is merely an extension of already established Martial Art techniques and abilities the use of the Internet is an extension of your Martial Arts Ministry.

What will it profit a man if he gains the whole world yet loses us soul? Worry not about the world, but on discipling those the Lord has entrust to you – impact their lives and you will impact the world.

Chapter 19: Stand Fast

Stand Strong, and Stand Fast in the Lord and the Power of His Might. (Gal. 5:1, 2 Thess. 2:15) So often Christians will look around and blame this one or that one – always making excuses instead of "Taking action for the Kingdom of God". The Scriptures are very clear that God hates just as He loves – God is perfectly balanced in all things.

It's important for us to stand fast and stand strong against wickedness, immorality, and any other thing that the Lord lets us know He hates. If we are burdened within our heart to share the love of God than it's important to remember to share an open rebuke when necessary. For an open rebuke may convict a person of their sin, causing them to repent and turn to God.

Furthermore as watchmen we have an obligation to make known to those around us the love of God in truth which means we also share with them the knowledge of what God hates.

Consider carefully the following list and teach your students how to stand against such things in a manner that gives glory to God.

Things God hates:

Homosexual acts (Leviticus 18:22).
Bestiality (Leviticus 18:23)
Idols, and the materials used to make idols (Deuteronomy 7:25)
Blemished sacrifices (Deuteronomy 17:1)
Worshipping the sun, moon or stars (Deuteronomy 17:3-4)
Witches, Divination, Astrology, Enchanters, (Deuteronomy 18:10)
Charmers, Wizards, Necromancers (Deuteronomy 18:11)
Transvestitism (Deuteronomy 22:5)

The Money of a whore
(Deuteronomy 23:18)
Remarriage to a former wife after
she has been married to another
man (Deuteronomy 24:4)
Dishonest scales (Deuteronomy
25:13-16)
Workers of iniquity (Psalm 5:5)
The wicked (Psalm 11:5)
Those who love violence (Psalm
11:5)
The perverse (Proverbs 3:32)
A proud look (Proverbs 6:16-17)
A lying tongue (Proverbs 6:17)
Hands that shed innocent blood
(Proverbs 6:17)
A heart that devises wicked
imaginations (Proverbs 6:18)
Feet that are swift in running to
mischief (Proverbs 6:18)
A false witness who speaks lies
(Proverbs 6:19)
Anyone who sows discord among
brethren (Proverbs 6:19)
Lying lips (Proverbs 12:22)
The sacrifices of the wicked
(Proverbs 15:8)

The ways of the wicked (Proverbs 15:9)
The thoughts of the wicked (Proverbs 15:26)
The proud in heart (Proverbs 16:5)
Those who justify the wicked (Proverbs 17:15)
Those who condemn the just (Proverbs 17:15)
Vain sacrifices (Isaiah 1:13)
Feasts as Israel celebrated them (Isaiah 1:14)
Robbery for burnt offering (Isaiah 61:8)
Idolatry (Jeremiah 44:2-4)
Evil plans against neighbors (Zechariah 8:17)
False oaths (Zechariah 8:17)
Esau (Malachi 1:1-3; Romans 9:13
Divorce (Malachi 2:14-16)
The deeds of the Nicolaitans (Revelation 2:6, 15)

Chapter 20: Conclusion

If you follow the guidance in this book you will be well on your way to starting a successful martial arts ministry that will have a real and practical impact in the lives of your students. Remember not to skip any steps in this book. All the topics that I've mentioned herein are of critical importance and leaving out one step may be detrimental to your aspirations of starting a martial arts ministry that glorifies God and makes disciples.

The foundation of this book comes from the Word of God and the principles therein. I encourage you this very day to start your journey – take a deep breath in and begin to seek the will of God in your life. I pray that the Lord would Bless you and your Martial Arts Ministry as you move forward in courage, faith and ultimately in love.

Special Gift

God has a Gift for You!   The Plan of Salvation:

There is no formal prayer of salvation as many churches would have you believe, God's Word is very clear - there is only one way to get to the Father in heaven and that is through Jesus Christ (John 14:6). Jesus says that you must be born again to enter into heaven (John 3:3-5).

Salvation is simply the first step in building an open and honest relationship with God. We all have sinned and fall short every day, but there is Hope in Jesus Christ - Just cry out to God in sincerity and honesty asking for forgiveness and for Him to Save you, Sanctify you, and fill you with His Holy Spirit - Ask for His will to be done in your life on earth as it is in Heaven and That's it, now just keep it real with God.

A Warning:

The Christian walk is not an easy life on the surface. The Word of God says that we will be hated in all the world for Christ namesake (Matt. 24:9). The Bible says that in the last days are enemy prevail against us physically until Christ returns to save us (Dan 7:21, 22). Furthermore, we must endure hardship as a good soldier of Jesus Christ (2 Tim 2:3) and yet we are never alone in this, God promises us that He will never leave us nor forsake us if we believe in him (Matt.28:20).

In everything we go through we have the peace and joy of God which surpasses all understanding (Philp. 4:6-8) The Bible declares, "For I consider the sufferings of this present time are not worthy to be compared with the glory which shall be revealed in us". (Rom 8:18). However, in all these things we are more than conquerors through Jesus Christ (Rom. 8:37)

Stay In Contact

Our Contact Information

Stay in Contact with the American Christian Defense Alliance, Inc. Contactus@acdainc.org Or Email Us Though Our Website At: www.ACDAInc.Org

Join Our Mailing List

We also Greatly Appreciate You Signing Up For Our Mailing List and Providing a Good Rating and review for this Book. Your reviews help other people like yourself find this book on Amazon and benefit from its contents.

If You or Your Family have been Blessed by this book please let us know by dropping us a line through our website at http://acdainc.org

Thanks Again for Reading

God Bless!

Our Books On Amazon

Our Books on Amazon:

Bible Studies for Belts: A Guide for Christian Martial Arts, Vol. 1: White Belt

Dirt on Your Tabies: 7 Short Stories of Seisho Ryu Ninjutsu

Biblical Bug Out: Don't Bug In - Follow The Calling

Christian Prepping 101: How To Start Prepping

Prepping: A Christian Perspective

Prepping: Survival Basics

Real Men Don't Make Promises: Understanding Oaths, Pacts, Covenants & Promises From A Biblical Perspective

Salvation for Your Unsaved Mom: 10 Things to Tell Your Mom Before She Dies